BECAUSE OF INDIA

Selected Poems and Fables

Suniti Namjoshi

Published in 1989 by ONLYWOMEN PRESS, Ltd.,
Radical Feminist and Lesbian publishers
38 Mount Pleasant, London WC1X 0AP, UK.

Some of these poems and fables have also appeared in the
following journals and anthologies: *Writers Workshop
Miscellany*, *Acta Victoriana*, *Descant*, *Scarborough Fair*,
Contemporary Verse Two, *Poetry Canada Review*,
Canadian Woman Studies, *GLC Women's Bulletin*, *New
Statesman*, *Trois*, and **Beautiful Barbarians** and **Ain't I a
Woman!**

Cover illustration © Geraldine Walsh.

Printed and bound by Nørhaven in Denmark.
Typeset by Columns of Reading, Berkshire, UK.

British Library Cataloguing in Publication Data
Namjoshi, Suniti, 1941–,
  Because of India: selected poems and fables.
  I. Title
  821

  ISBN 0-906500-33-8

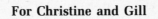

For Christine and Gill

CONTENTS

Poems (Calcutta: Writers Workshop, 1967)

As I began the task of selecting the poems for this book, I couldn't help remembering the various contexts in which they were written. It occurred to me that some explanation might serve a useful purpose, at least to make clear that it's only possible to think and feel what the language and concepts available at any particular point in time allow.

When my first book of poems was published in 1967, I was just very pleased, the pleasure was uncomplicated. I had no idea how lucky I had been, or how fortunate it was for me that P. Lal of the Writers Workshop was giving Indian poets who wrote in English a chance to get their work into print. These poems were written between 1964–66. I had been selected for the Indian Administrative Service in 1964, and my mother's family had seen to it that I was posted in Poona, where they lived. Their farms were about 65 miles away in another district. I had worked extremely hard for the competitive exam for the I.A.S., because it seemed to me that that was my only chance of being somebody in my own right and gaining some independence from the family. But it hadn't worked out that way. Though, on the whole, the family was scrupulous about not asking me to do favours for friends, relatives and clients, I was nonetheless perceived by the local community as a member of that particular family and tended to inherit their friends and enemies. As a rule this worked out in my favour, rather than otherwise.

The I.A.S. itself was fascinating: I met lawyers, farmers, landowners, tenants, civil servants and politicians and learnt a little bit about what they wanted and how they worked to get it. It was also disappointing. I.A.S. probationers tend to think rather well of themselves, because they are among the selected few. It took me a while to realise that someone educated in English was obviously more likely to do well in an exam conducted in English than someone educated in one of the regional languages. I've often thought that had I been a better person, I'd have stayed on in the I.A.S. and tried to improve things. But I've also thought that had I been a worse person I'd have stayed on in the I.A.S., not done anything, not rocked the boat, and grown senior simply by virtue of growing older. In the two years I served as an Assistant Collector, what I actually did was compromise. I was honest. I did the work set before me. But I didn't do anything more. And once I had figured out how to stay out of trouble, I grew bored.

I thought that now that I had managed more or less to become somebody, I could perhaps take up writing verse. I seemed to want to. On the other hand, I thought, many young people want to be poets or artists or something romantic of the sort, and surely the probability is that most of them have no talent. It is, therefore, likely that I too have no talent. Having delivered this little speech to myself, I decided to give myself a year at writing verse and then see what I thought, and then another year, and another. . . It's perhaps fortunate that when one is bad, one has little notion of what it is that isn't good enough. Perhaps the best thing is to believe that one is bad, but not bad enough to give up; and also that one is good, but not so good that one can't improve. So I wrote for 20 minutes or more a day and inflicted the results on whoever I thought would be sympathetic.

There was one thing that the I.A.S. did for me for which I have always been grateful: it absolutely forced me to read Marathi, since a considerable proportion of the office work was in Marathi. Though Marathi is supposed to be my mother tongue, I hadn't actually ever been taught to read and write it. When I was posted to my home state, I wasn't going to admit that. So I combined my verbal knowledge of Marathi with my written knowledge of Hindi and managed as best I could. It was during this period that I did some translations from old Marathi poetry with my mother and grandmother, and of some modern Marathi poetry with my mother. That helped, but I wish now that while I still lived in India, I had read more Marathi.

Meanwhile, my verse lurched on. I was an Assistant Collector, a Sub-divisional Magistrate, my family was pleased with me. I was no longer fighting them over a particular friend. The word "lesbian" had not been thrown around and it wasn't in my own active vocabulary. I think now, after all these years, that in the end the basic message from the family was, "Well, all right, do what you like, but BE DISCREET." That's why I've included the poem with the police imagery in this selection – there's a knowledge in it that there are some rules it would be foolhardy to break. I certainly didn't think that the police were my enemy. Indeed, one of my jobs was to maintain law and order. Surely I must have assumed that I was about as Establishment as it was possible to be. And yet, and yet, the poem reveals a certain unease.

THE HEAD OF THE ROSE

Quietly we said, "My friend, you have talent."
Left unsaid the ordinary things,
A honeysuckle cottage, chequered tablecloths.
And the feelers we put out, just as other people do,
Twisted and met with tough grace.
What creed was it we affirmed or denied?
Oh I think the Mughal emperor
Built that tomb before her death,
Seeing the black holes in the bright summer.
Was it courage or fear that kept us silent
Watching the dragonfly over the water?
Now I give you the head of the rose.

(1965–66)

VARIOUS REASONS

A policeman? He raised his hand? So,
He said, "Stop." But is that poetry?
Is that life? Now there are no policemen
In my mind, neither traffic, nor otherwise,
Tho' of course it's natural to assume,
But stone walls do not a prison make,
And by upbringing and birth I'm not a citizen
Of a police state. Not that I hate policemen
And they don't really remind me of anything;
But the policeman said, "Stop."
And, my dear, they do exist.

(1965–66)

ONCE I SAW

Once I saw the Ganges in the morning
And almost knew then why they called her
  "mother",
Those others come to Kashi to be cleansed.
We played upon the bank with bows and arrows,
We three alone, my brothers and I,
Never thinking that the throng in the temple
Was us, never guessing that the corpse
In the river was us. We played. That was all
Till the boatman ferried us over, where
The weavers lived and worked, and seeing ourselves
In the looms, we knew our kinship then.

(1965–66)

AT NIGHT

Listen heart,
The small sounds,
Insect life.
There's the rustling inside.
The rustle of silk?
My breath caught
Till I shrugged
And went back to sleep.

(1965–66)

More Poems (Calcutta: Writers Workshop, 1971)

In 1968 I managed to get study leave from the Government of India to go to the United States to do a master's in Public Administration at the University of Missouri. The logic of lesbianism figured in "Pinocchio" had its literal outcome: I did indeed move "to the other side of the curtain." In Columbia, Missouri I had a severe case of culture shock. To understand the language, but not the context, is extremely unnerving. Briefly, the problem was that I thought the natives were barbaric, but they seemed to think that they were going to civilise me. I had begun to question the values of certain members of the society I was used to in poems like "The Little Chapel" for example, but didn't really think much of the American alternative I was presented with. This was also my first experience of racism. It took me two or three months to recognise it for what it was. After that I became vicious, that is, I carried a verbal knife around with me. I reacted to being looked down upon with a superior brand of snobbery, with remarks like 'Americans don't know the first thing about real snobbery,' and with a determination to beat them at their own game. No, not at snobbery, at English Literature. I had an uneasy suspicion that this was foolish, that this was a course that must be pursued with reservations. After all, the last thing I wanted to do was become one of them; but a clear analysis required the politicization that only occurred years later.

One aspect of culture shock is that one is not recognised – in both senses of the word. In India I was inescapably my grandfather's granddaughter, one member of a particular family located for hundreds of years in a particular region, with a particular place in a particular system. I was free of all that. But now I was literally Nobody from Nowhere – and I didn't like it. This was the tail end

14

of the sixties. I had some friends among radical students who were in the SDS (Students for a Democratic Society). Their politics astonished me. They weren't particularly feminist – not that I was ready for feminism yet – and if anything, they were vaguely contemptuous of lesbians, which did little to endear their ideas to me or to help me in working out my own.

THE LITTLE CHAPEL

When I am old and rich and gracious,
I shall have a little chapel in my garden,
And every morning I shall walk there,
Checking the red roses and white.
I shall always pray in a white sari —
White is so becoming to prayer.
In the mornings I shall pray,
In the evenings pour tea.
And all the gracious ladies in the city
Will envy my tea ceremony.
And my old bones will lie comforted
With the elegance of my white sari
And my elegant porcelain.

(1966–67)

PINOCCHIO

And if I spoke to you, what would I say?
That there's a change? That I can still feel the
    ground
Shifting and giving under my feet?
That you are made of ivory and steel
And very beautiful, and I'm afraid
To smudge the miracle with my fingertips?
I'm content to look in the moonlight,
To parody my own wonder, to wear
A powdered mask – how white the mask in the
    moonlight –
And turn cartwheels about you. Oh be a ghost
In the moonlight, be a dream. That you should be
    real
Terrifies me. Don't move. Don't speak.
If you speak let your words be contained in the veil.
My face is a mask in the moonlight. I'm a doll
made of brown wood. My features never change.
If you are a doll carved in ivory,
We may – it is permitted – dance
A minuet in the moonlight. But don't,
I beg you, don't slip. If we should stumble
And clutching one another, discover
We're neither wood nor ivory, they'd switch on
The lights and the children would scream
And we would have to move
To the other side of the curtain.

                                        (1966–67)

17

THOSE ASTONISHING ANGLO-SAXONS

Somebody said:
> Here is a country
> With all the amenities,
> Land of free air, water to drink,
> One wild beast,
> The horrid grizzly bear,
> Two dread snakes, the python and the rattle,
> Indians and squaws,
> 'Quakes' and tornadoes.
> Go forth and live.
They did.

(1968–69)

COLUMBIA, AMERICA

In Columbia, America,
The little houses grow,
White, sometimes yellow,
All in a row.
The trees are orderly,
The squirrels discreet,
And the only jarring note
Is a bird in bad taste
Lying dead on the street.
Accidents will happen.

(1968–69)

AMONG THE GIGGLING CHILDREN

Among the giggling children
(Who are charming in their freshness)
I stand with the night in my eyes,
And they wonder
That the long slope of night
Is gentle
And leads to you.

(1968–69)

Cyclone in Pakistan (Calcutta: Writers Workshop, 1971)

In 1969 I resigned from the Indian Administrative Service, and went to McGill University to do a Ph.D. They had given me a teaching assistantship, and had agreed, after some hesitation, that a third master's degree wasn't really necessary. From my point of view, McGill was a great improvement. Montreal was cosmopolitan, I was doing literature again and the culture shock was dissipating. This was still the early seventies. Some of the radicalism of the students rubbed off, though most of it didn't make much sense to me. I came across almost nothing in the way of feminism or gay liberation. Ginsberg did a reading there once. I was shocked. As poems like "Nov. 1970 'CYCLONE IN PAK.'" indicate, I was acquiring the beginnings of a social conscience, or perhaps it was only a social consciousness. The real teaching experience had to do with feeling in my lived life what it was like to be poor to the point of wondering what one was going to eat. There was also the matter of experiencing the social hierarchy at the bottom end of the system.

Meanwhile, my ear for poetry was improving. I was fortunate in that I did most of my work under Louis Dudek, who was a poet as well as an academic. I wanted to write my doctoral dissertation on Ezra Pound, on the basis of the **Selected Poems** I had come across in India. Dudek suggested I work on "Ezra Pound and Reality: The Metaphysics of the Cantos". I hadn't read **The Cantos** and I wasn't particularly interested in the metaphysics. I had wanted to learn from Pound's versification. What can I say? Reader, I did it! The odd thing is that though aestheticism enabled me to ignore Pound's politics, Pound's own insistence that economics and politics are definitely within the province of

21

the poet, stayed in my mind. As a Hindu living in India, anti-Semitism hadn't been an issue in the forefront of my experience . Even so, my ability to persist in spite of Pound's anti-Semitism seems to me now as astonishing as my ability to overlook the male-centred consciousness of the literature I was studying.

Once, in one of the seminars, someone made a remark about what would have happened if the Germans had won the war. I shrugged and said that as far as I was concerned, all it would have meant was that I'd have been a student of German Literature rather than of English Literature. I hadn't meant to shock at all, but it was evident I had succeeded. 'If a small island hadn't conquered the world. . .' I found myself thinking. It was the beginnings of a notion of cultural clout.

Perhaps, it was also the beginning of the notion of an Asian perspective, an alien perspective, later a lesbian perspective. I remember that the anti-Vietnam War students in Missouri baffled me at first. Why wouldn't someone want to fight for their country? Next I thought they were gloriously moral for not wanting to shed blood. Finally I realised that it wasn't a question of fighting for their country at all. There was one perception I had, though, which wasn't voiced by anyone I knew. This was that whoever was fighting whoever else and for whatever cause, the country which always suffered most was the country they were fighting about and fighting on.

GILL AND HIS MERMAID

A woman in a gilded sarong said,
'Now for the first time in your life
you live. The palm trees are real,
the sand is real and I am real.
I have made this possible.'
But one day she died
and there was only a great dead fish
on the shore which wasn't quite real anymore.

(1968–69)

CULMINATIONS

Haven't you heard? They say
the nations are merging
black, red, brown, white,
green, yellow, purple, blue,
like spinning confetti
on carnival day.

(1969)

CONTEMPORARY

The government official
speaks in English with friends,
in Hindi with servants,
and reserves his mother tongue
for his 2 Alsatian dogs.

(1969–70)

Nov. 1970 'CYCLONE IN PAK.'

100,000 human beings
were swallowed by sea
in a single day
and then thrown up,
because
2000 miles of polluted oil
have made the sea
less than tolerant.
"Think of the loss," they said,
"visualize in numbers.
Sea-sodden corpses
are useful to no one.
200,000 eyeballs
never to be grafted.
100,000 heads of hair
spoilt by sea water.
Next time it happens
we'll have a freezer handy.
Next time a battery
of poets will be ready."

(1970)

The Jackass and the Lady (Calcutta: Writers Workshop, 1980)

In 1972 I got a job teaching English Literature at Scarborough College, University of Toronto. I had worked terribly hard on my doctoral dissertation, and by comparison the desultory fashion in which I had been trying to write verse appeared laughable. If writing a dissertation on a poet was so hard, then how much harder was the task of learning to be a good poet. I started writing, that is sitting at a desk and scribbling, 4 hours a day, 6 days a week. The 4 hours came first, and then the academic work required of me. It was made clear to me that I had been hired because I had a Ph.D. in English Literature, and not because I wanted to write verse. "Don't we all write occasional verse?" a colleague murmured.

Most of the poems in **The Jackass and the Lady** were written between 1972–1976. When I came up for tenure in 1976 I was allowed to submit the manuscript for consideration, but only in addition to academic articles. Colleagues, as members of an institution, subscribed to the rules of the institution; colleagues, as friends, were sometimes sympathetic. An offer of publication by a small Canadian Press fell through, and so the book wasn't published till 1980. By 1980 I was a feminist, and revised some of the poems accordingly. In some instances it was simply a matter of restoring the poems to their original form. For example, I had given the poem, "I give her the rose," the title "The Unicorn" in a rather muddled attempt at subterfuge. In other instances, for example in the poem about the upside down swan, I boldly turned "he" into "she" even though I had had "he" originally.

During this period I was enchanted by the literary universe of Northrop Frye and by the poetry of Jay Macpherson. And though I didn't know either of them personally, I did attend Frye's lectures in one of his graduate courses. I used to sneak into the back of the auditorium quietly. It seemed to me though that there was no place for me in this humanist universe, except perhaps as one of the helpful animals in the mode of romance.

Looking back on these poems, I think what happened was an unconscious and not entirely happy confluence of Western and Hindu influences. Here's the epigraph I made up for Section III of *The Jackass and the Lady*:

Neither snake, nor prince, nor charmer,
> but the baffled fool for my lady in green
> in the well-known forest.

Well, I wasn't the prince. And I wasn't having any of the snake business — I suspect the Hindu background was too strong for that. I should say here that I wasn't brought up at all as an orthodox Hindu; but if one grows up in a Hindu family in India, however liberal, then certain ways of thinking that are characteristically Hindu seep in through the pores so to speak. And I certainly wasn't the lady, though I was beginning to question gender stereotyping (at the time I didn't know that was what it was called). That left only the beast. But here, I think, the Hindu influence operates again. To me a beast wasn't "bestial" in the Western sense. To me a bird or a beast was a creature like anyone else. Hinduism is, after all, pantheistic; and the popular notion of reincarnation attributes a soul to everyone. This may sound odd to Western ears, but for me, it was as familiar as it was unconscious. It was in the very air I had breathed while growing up.

Now, years later, I think I was heading towards the same perceptions by a roundabout way as those being voiced by some Western feminists today. It's apparent to many women that in a humanist universe, which has been male-centred historically,

28

women are "the other", together with the birds and the beasts and the rest of creation. An identification with the rest of creation, possibly with the whole of it, would only be logical; unless, of course, one wished to create a mirror image of the humanist universe, with woman at the centre, accepting the consequences of consigning everything else to "the other". But I don't want to be separated from the birds and the beasts, nor do I want to "humanise" them particularly. (It should be said that as far as I can understand it, Frye's Anagogic Man includes rather than excludes. But surely the demonic version of this is that he eats up everything instead of letting things be?)

All this complicated process still left one question unresolved. All right, I was a beast, a creature. But what sort of beast was I?

ALICE

It is evident, therefore, that the chief distinction
between the lakes and the sea is that the sea is
inclusive, but does not reflect. (*Manual of Oceano-
logy, 1973*). "And the human eye?" she asked.
"That," said the rabbit rather pontifically, "is less
than the ocean and more than the lakes."

What seashells flourish in sand, undersea,
in the cool element where the timid drown?

> Alice goes crazy staring at mirrors.
> I loved her once. Alice goes crazy.
> Watch the tide. I have not displaced
> the hard glass. Watch the tide.

Don't you dream anymore?

> That the gull returns coloured by the blood
> the setting sun sheds, that mariners speak
> of a sea of light, that you wished to bathe
>   in seamless green?

I see you what you are:
> gull and mourner
> on a glass sea.

(1972–73)

AND SHE WROTE HER POEMS

And she wrote her poems because muteness
                    terrified her,
seeing, as she did, in the level lake water
                        an upside down swan.

(1972–73)

I GIVE HER THE ROSE

I give her the rose with unfurled petals.
She smiles
        and crosses her legs.
I give her the shell with the swollen lip.
She laughs. I bite
        and nuzzle her breasts.
I tell her, "Feed me on flowers
        with wide open mouths,"
and slowly,
        she pulls down my head.

(1974–75)

HOMAGE TO CIRCE

*. . . this frame wee looke upon hath beene upon our
trenchers; in briefe, we have devoured ourselves.*
Religio Medici I, 37

She rewards her lovers at random
    like Circe feeding tit-bits to mice,
    almonds to bears,
           and whatever's handy
to miscellaneous swine.

The snake curled about Circe's shoulder
    tracing the whorl of her perfect ear
        with an agile tongue.

The little dog barked,
was a good little dog,
        burrowed
its nose in her warm thighs.
The dog, who barked
        and laughed,
had bright eyes.

I am all animals to you?
I could sit cat-like and gaze
        sisterly.

I am all animals to you,
        could offer myself
          on a wide lily-pad,
drink from your cup and eat from your lip,
turn bird for your purpose, feed
from your hand – disarm the wary.
She draws the birds from the trees,
they would say, she tames the hungry.

                    Circle,
all animals adore you,
you are all things to each
in the tutelary garden, at the continuous feast.
                                        (1974–75)

THE ANIMALS IN THIS FOREST

"The animals in this forest are incorrigibly friendly."
    But do I like you then? I do not so.
            The cat has her kittens
            and the dog has his day.
            Be civil and play
                     before winter comes.
"Why do beasts inhabit your mind?"
        They like it there.
I thought I could please disguised
                as a swallow.
As a fox I was groomed, my manners
                were good
and my wits were keen. As a fish
                I glittered.
But bird, beast and fish is all that
                I am.
And therefore:
            Do I like you then?
                I do not so.
And bird, beast and fish is all my theme.

                          (1974–75)

THE JACKASS AND THE LADY

I *Festina Lente*

Gold coin hung in a childish sky
is this a season as mild as milk?
        Here there are dragons,
an untrodden bridge, a snow-white
jackass. The dragons submerge
in the pale water, but where is the lady?
The lady is naked and has no spurs.
The jackass laughs.
    "Please to proceed with dispassionate
haste." The lady shifts. The jackass
grins. The sun canters.

II *The Misgivings of the Jackass*

To mince among corpses
      is not that our delight?
To smile with precision
      our constant preoccupation?
Fish float, cats laugh,
      and we amble cautiously,
while a silly sun simpers
      and solicits the moon.

The later poems in the Jackass series are no longer extant, but tradition has it that in the final episode the jackass and the lady part company. The lady ascends to more spiritual realms. The jackass wallows in its own emotion. All this occurs amidst stellar applause.

That is all that is known with any certainty about the jackass and the lady. There is, however, a fragmentary drawing. In this drawing the jackass is couchant (lying on its back) and the lady ascendant (as indicated earlier). There are stars in the sky. But what makes this drawing particularly suspect is the fact that the jackass is depicted with a sword in its heart. Now, the extreme sentimentality of such a posture is not in keeping with the tone of the poems. Under the picture are three lines of verse, usually referred to as the Jackass' Farewell:

Throw away the flesh, the skin and the guts,
but keep the bone of admiration
in stasis on your shelf.

These lines have hitherto been regarded as apocryphal, but Professor Jackworthy's new interpretation has done much of late to give them greater credence. The sword, he feels, is the lady's parting gift. The use of the colour red indicates clearly that the dead jackass continues to live. The purpose of the sword is to enable the creature to shed its skin, its shaggy exterior. The professor is now engaged in an intensive search for the missing parchment. He feels reasonably certain that the drawing, when found, will depict the jackass cheerfully restored to its human form.

IV *Fragment from the Jackass MS.*

edited by S. Jackworthy

Canticle to the Sun

The earth is a round ball.
I am a jackass.
You are a rich boy. You live
next door. Come play with me?
Your insolence is appalling.
You shed your lustre
with extreme indifference, and you caress
my naked lady without a hint of rivalry.

(Translated by S. Jackworthy)

V *The Epitaph of the Jackass*

Daylight and broken mouth
   in the short grass shards.
                Underneath all
5000 bones
   – both elegant and enchanting.

                       (1974–75)

The Authentic Lie (U. of New Brunswick: Fiddlehead Poetry Books now called Goose Lane Editions, 1982)

Most of these poems were written between 1976–1978, and the manuscript was ready before my 1978–79 sabbatical leave; but once again an offer from a Canadian publisher fell through. That is why though **Feminist Fables** was written later, it was published earlier.

"Discourse with the Dead" has to do with my father's death. He was a test pilot and was killed in a plane crash on 11 Dec. 1953. I was twelve at the time; but because of boarding schools, I was only eleven when I last saw him. ("Discourse with the Dead" says I was ten, because "eleven" has too many syllables in it.) For years after his death I had a recurrent dream, with variations, about how he hadn't really been killed, only lost, and had come back again. **The Authentic Lie** is an attempt to deal with the child's grief which had never been dealt with properly. Section II of the book, "The Assassins" examines gratuitous killing, whether literal or metaphorical. And Section III, "The Authentic Lie" concludes that one can't really follow the dead beyond a certain point if one is alive.

I'm not sure what the political implications of all this are for me as a feminist. I loved my father. I also liked him. For the child, for his daughter, his only crime was that he died. For the woman writing the poems, the central task was to clarify and shape the raw material of the grief of the child. At the time I wasn't a feminist, in the sense that I had no understanding of patriarchy as an institution. Later, in **From the Bedside Book of Nightmares**, I tried to deal with the implications of feminism for my family loyalties. Prospero, in "Snapshots of Caliban", is certainly a patriarchal figure, and not a pleasant one. The figure in "Misfit" in **Feminist**

41

Fables is a kindly, though unsatisfactory patriarch, based on a distant and very rough similarity to a grandfather I also loved. And in "From Baby F With Much Love" I say explicitly, "We loved those kindly gentlemen. . ." (**From the Bedside Book of Nightmares**). Perhaps what's relevant here is my earlier remark about colleagues as members of an institution, and colleagues as individuals and friends. Members of an institution tend, at least officially, to subscribe to the rules of the institution.

Once I found I could deal with my father's death, it occurred to me that I could also try to grapple with another problem that had been vexing me for some time. It was, to put it simply: how to write about India in English. After all, my Indian experience was as everyday and as familiar to me as anything could be; but in English, things Indian became exotic. I thought, rather despairingly, that my father's death was so personal that perhaps it was universal. 'After all,' I said to myself, 'I needn't actually say that the sea I was thinking of was the Arabian Sea.' The problem is probably most acute in lyric poetry, which relies heavily on a frame of reference. Perhaps it's more easily dealt with in extended works of fiction, which allow more room for description. But my mind doesn't work that way.

DISCOURSE WITH THE DEAD

I
No, do not trouble.
    All my lost loves
are quite recovered,
        have been seen
at parties, are witty and well.

He died when she was ten in a distant country
and therefore the dreams wouldn't stop.

She made nightly journeys,
                climbed out of bed,
walked to the shore.
                Who is that sleeping giant?
Not your father – of his bones
                are coral made.
She examined his body – his gills
                    were slits –
then heaved him up quickly
                    on the palm
of one hand
            (like a gigantic balloon,
            like a bloated whale)
                hurried home with him.

First a live man,
  then a dead man:
          Where is my father?
In the sky, a personal star,
                    shedding
effulgence.

While you were lost in the forest
   we lived in the world.
Why don't you come back,
                       walking
towards us, by chance, as it were,
                             covered
with tendrils?

You are too sinister
to welcome. Year after year
the corpse rots quietly. That dream
undergoes a slow surface change,
the texture is different.
                          I fear your presence.

After your death we grew up
more or less. Life – is miscellaneous,
but nonetheless dazzling. There's rust
on the surface. I mention it briefly.

Follow, follow – how easy
            is it then – over
the edge and down the cliff.
        That extended fall –
you and I floating
                in unhurried ease.

II
That dream is a hook,
        it hauls us both
to that dreary no-place,
            where
loss is no-loss,
        and your tiredness
failure.

In the morning a miracle,
a whale on the beach, its head
pointed north, neatly laid out.
It's probably dying. A whale
in shallow water is destined
to drown – the lungs collapse.
It starts rotting.

Send them away, those who shriek,
those who wheel, and those who dive
like gulls for love. Their need
and greed and bodies drive them.
Gulls are scavengers.

Here, sit on this bank and watch
the silver fish, who do not throw back
their heads and sing, who float
unconcerned, and are probably stupid.

No monsters perturb
            the uncertain depths.
There's nothing down there,
            only black water.

Roll back the rock.
   Examine the cave.
The body is gone,
      but the soul remains,
           trailing terror.

And at the core, the intrepid worm:
        it burrowed to the centre,
        made its own darkness,
        discovered corruption
                in wild surmise.

III

Slips from the hand of God
        the simple soul, without
        any clothes on, and without colour.

Once, in a cave, Mama Bear licked
                    this lump into shape.

The kid is dead.
                    Go up and down
the house, up and down the house.
Whom did you meet? I met the kid
                    on its private errands.

"Race you to the end." Brown grass. Dazzling day. So we run across the field. Colossus not standing, but Colossus running: I like that better. Am astounded to discover that adults can run.

And you don't remember, but I remember. When we lived by the sea, there was a storm one day: the waves reared up and the rain beat down. All that afternoon there was a storm and I watched it. You wouldn't let me go out and play in it.

And another time we almost flew to the moon. It got bigger and bigger, but it was late in the evening and so we went home. And once we flew through some clouds. I expected revelation, but nothing happened.

I remember that I would jump from heights and that you would catch me. Remember also that I would jump into the pool and follow instructions, would go down like a plummet and come up like a cork, holding my breath rather patiently, I thought, till you swam up to me and fished me out.

I remember a good bit – one promise you didn't keep. (You said we could go duck-shooting and we never went.) And once you were angry. A man had let his cows stray into the garden and you shouted at him. That was unusual. Saw you do something very silly too. It was a joke. You pretended there was a mouse in the box and the European ladies screamed. I didn't say anything, but I suppose I must have looked disapproving. And once you told me a persuasive half-lie; but that's the list of my charges and quickly torn up, or, if remembered, then remembered only for scraps of memory.

No hurt, no hate, no uncivil circumstance:
that corpse was given a seemly farewell. . .

Then why do I grieve? Not honest. What I never forgave you for was being less than a god, for being hopelessly mortal. Never mind. That's accounting and quibbling. But what am I doing? Trying to resurrect the dead? It's all a part of living probably. And the dead are very patient, they are endlessly patient with those who live now.

IV

Your father had a father. . .
That improves nothing, makes matters worse.

Stun the sun, seek out his blood;
        those faded energies
go unavenged, and Time the droll troll
crouches on your chest
           dribbling.

Some day the giddy motion
of the circular sun must come
to an end. The sun must halt
and examine his work. But the sun
is blind. Throw a spear at the sun,
falls off his shield. Sling a stone
at the sun to bloody his eye. The sun
is made of metal and can't be killed.

But if the sun were mortal, then what would
happen?

A sun rises, a callow sun,
              and a horseman goes riding
straight across the plain.
              The sun is slaughtered.
A sun rises, a buoyant sun,
              and a horseman goes riding
straight across the plain. . .
                    Astounding resurrections,
repetitive deaths: what they mean
                    I do not know.
That gay lancer, Death,
              and his crony, the sun, joust every day.

Death's close embrace, not longed for,
not sought as such. The thing is,
of course, that Death is a skeleton,
his bones my own.

To die free and easy, to insure
with surcease a kind of success, a smiling
release... The piety of daughters
is hard to endure.

V

That lunatic fish lured to the shore
by my persistent howling.

The sea was made of glass,
the sun just risen, and the fish
glittered, breathing painfully.
I set him in the sea.

But you were always drowning,
bobbing in the sea. If you shook back the waves
and strode to the shore, what could you say
and still not deceive? 'Wicked, wicked, wicked,'
that's the waves' complaint. 'To say that the dead
are indeed the dead is not to kill.' Those
yellow dog waves, they're lounging on the shore,
they're licking your feet.

Consider now the giant father
        and his no less giant daughter
wading in the sea. Do they leave
or approach? Is that sunrise
               or sunset?
Leave them to their occupation,
        they are happy enough,
handsome enough, further beatitude
left to other hands, a farther future.

                      (1976–77)

THREE STEPS

I *Statement*

This willingness to kill
          – sudden, inexplicable.

II *Preferences*

How
would you like your death?
Death that is borne on a wasp's wings?
Death that is planted under your skin
                    and shatters like glass
on a hard high note and you die
breathlessly more or less consigning
                    your atoms to air?
Or substantial death? When you dream
that you are dreaming and lift
a mastodon and your fantastic
dream goes ping, goes pop,
                    and the mastodon
falls, and you lie there crushed
                    tasting yourself?
(Death by drowning is simple-minded
                    bliss.)
And then there's the death in the eyes
                    of your friend.
His knife or yours, doesn't matter
                    much.
This death thrills. The nerves sing.

III *Harangue, or What One Poet Said to Another*

We live in an age of abdicating Hamlets, and
the voices of poetry are princely disclaimers: It is
not I, I, I. . . It's an age that believes that admission
of guilt for a crime not known may possibly lead to
absolution from guilt. It is not that we are innocent.
We do not claim innocence. We are willing to be
punished. We are punished, but we'd like to file a
statement of the most astounding and abysmal
ignorance. Meanwhile, of course, the gunmen mock.
They acknowledge the killer. They shout with
exuberance, "It is I, I, I." It was said long ago: you
can kill and kill and still be a hero – thus Macbeth.
Then you cannot anymore. Be a hero, I mean. If
society tells you that you're not a killer, it's still a
lie. Lies, like beauty are only skin-deep. Go meet
the killer behind your eyelids. Until you do, you
will kill and kill and kill yet again, and still not
admit that you committed murder. Then will you
kill? You probably will. And your next protagonist
will be a gunman, straight from the tabloids, Son of
Sam. Novel lies. Ingenuous liars.

(1976–77)

GLASS COFFINS

There were two glass coffins, the prince was in one and Snow-White was in the other, and though the sun glared and the leaves fell, the glass was undamaged. They were like pretty marionettes in cellophane wrappers waiting to live. And the dwarfs were not miners, they were cybernetic experts, wise wiremen doing their damnedest to trigger the dream. Then a thought leaped an arc. A sudden impulse: "Cough up that apple." Snow-White coughs. "Break through the glass." Her fist crashes. The dream begins. Stepping so gingerly, so timidly on grass she approaches the prince. He has snow-white hair. This is no prince. This is the king. He died in his sleep. She buries him. Then "Cough up that apple." Snow-White coughs. "Break through the glass." Had she time to consider, she might prefer not to dream.

(1976–77)

RED KING TO ALICE

Can the dead mourn the dead?
                    What did you want?
You dreamt the dream.
                    I understood
nothing. My body failed.
                    In the dream you were
queen and lived at the top
                    of a tall tower.
I fell from this tower. You shouted
                    out loud.
We looked down at once.
                    I was probably dead.
But the bones came together. The body
                    moved.
It scrabbled at the wall. The body
                    struggled.
It slithered up the side of your tall
                    wall.
A hand gripped the ledge. The legs
                    followed.
The head gaped.
                    And you toppled from the top
of your tall tower. I shouted
                    out loud.
We looked down at once,
                    but probably in vain.

(1976–77)

LUNATIC BEAST

Someone was dead. Somebody
shouted. "Don't let go." But she did
let go, and possibly she died, or dreamed
that she did. The sun started spinning
and the sea was a large and lunatic beast.
It roared. It was noisy. She started laughing.

(1976–77)

Feminist Fables (London: Sheba Feminist
Publishers, 1981)

In 1978–79 I was given my first sabbatical
leave. I spent the first six or seven months in
London and the rest in Cambridge. In London I met
lesbians and gay men – as part of a community
rather than as isolated individuals – for the first
time. I went to Sappho, I went to the Gateways and
I was very lonely. Cambridge was better. I made
friends there; but it was Christine Donald who was
particularly important to me and who began to
politicize me. I put up a great resistance and a great
many arguments, but also felt enormously relieved
to find that I wasn't isolated in my questioning of
the prevailing order. Christine was both patient
and, of course, intelligent, and had a literary
sensibility that I could respect.

What isn't clear to me is why I wasn't
influenced by feminism earlier. In the early days at
Scarborough College I had one colleague who was a
strong feminist. She recommended Stein and Duras
to me. Somehow nothing much happened. Perhaps
I wasn't ready. Perhaps it was because her primary
literary interests weren't centred on poetry. Perhaps
it was because she was too American and I was too
Indian. I hadn't properly understood the structures
of Western society, or even of my own. I remember
making one remark that still troubles me. It went
something like this: "Here in the West, all that
seems to matter for social status is gender and
money. But in India several other factors operate:
caste, class and family background. An Indian
woman who has all these factors operating for her
certainly isn't oppressed. And it seems to me that
such women are far less awkward and far more
assured than many of the women I've seen here."
There's more than one kind of stupidity in this
remark. First, there's the tendency to regard being

oppressed as somehow ignoble. But what really appals me now is my utter disregard of the women who had all the factors operating against them.

It's ironic that in December 1980 when I went to India full of eagerness to explain feminist ideas to my mother, her instant response was to the effect: "I'm damned if I see myself as an oppressed woman!" I knew she wouldn't like the gay liberation ideas much; but I had thought that, as a strong-minded and independent woman, she would take to feminist ideas like a duck to water.

It wasn't just Christine's intellect that was persuasive. It was watching her be brave and get hurt. She wore feminist and gay liberation badges, and sometimes there would be frighteningly aggressive arguments and remarks from men on the street. It shamed me that I was letting other women do the fighting for me. I don't like being an activist. It frightens me, it doesn't suit my temperament, I dislike arguments; but when I returned to Toronto I came out at the university and in print, and, together with some women colleagues, I started a Women's Studies Programme at the college.

During the sabbatical leave, which was about 14 months, including the summer holidays, I produced no usable work, though I read a great deal. Christine had started me out on an elementary work on feminism, then Millett's **Sexual Politics**, then Adrienne Rich's work and so on. When I returned to Toronto in August 1979, I began writing **Feminist Fables**. They were done by December 1980 and published in 1981. For me, they were a way of exploring feminist ideas and their implications for the patterns I had inherited through the mainstream literary tradition. The knowledge that an audience existed to whom I would make sense made all the difference. It released my imagination to try to make the patterns that were authentic to me.

THE WICKED WITCH

A rather handsome young dyke strode through the forest and knocked at the door of a small house, which belonged to a witch. The witch answered the door, and the dyke said, "I'm sorry to bother you, but I've come on a quest. I have a question and had hoped you could help me." The witch considered for a moment, then asked her in. She made some tea. "What is your question?" asked the witch. "What is the Real Thing?" "What?" "That is my question," answered the dyke. "I fell in love with a beautiful woman, and though she professed some affection for me, she assured me nonetheless that what I felt for her was not the Real Thing." "And did you ask her her meaning?" "Yes," said the dyke. "She said that the love between a man and a woman is the Real Thing." "I see," said the witch. "Well, here are your choices. Turn into a man, go to this woman, and say to her this time, 'Look, I'm a man, and therefore capable of the Real Thing.'" "No," said the dyke, "I'm not a man. How can an unreal person feel a real thing?" "Well then," said the witch, "get 500 people to go to this woman and say to her loudly that, in their opinion, what you feel for her is the Real Thing." "No," said the dyke, "I feel what I feel. What difference does it make what other people say they think I feel?" "It helps," shrugged the witch. "It's known as the Principle of Corroborative Reality. However, here's your third choice. Forget other people and find out for yourself what you really feel." "I see," said the dyke. "And when and where and how shall I begin?" "Now?" said the witch and poured tea.

(1979–80)

COMPLAINT

Two knights in a forest. It's early in May. Bright sunlight filters through the leaves. A damsel in distress is weeping quietly. One of the knights has abducted this damsel. The other is her lover. The knights are fighting. Her lover wins. But the problem is that the damsel in distress has already been raped. The knight, her lover, is greatly distressed. How can he marry her? He grieves bitterly.

(1979–80)

THE SAURIAN CHRONICLES

Two lizards on a rock are sunning themselves. It's early in October. The rains have just stopped. The younger lizard, wishing to be amiable, says to the elder, "O wisest of lizards, O long-lived one, tell me once again – if you think it is proper – of the world's beginning." The Old Lizard's tongue flickers for a moment. Her eyes cloud over. She opens her eyes and begins. "Know then, that the sun is a lizard, a fire-breathing dragon, and the earth is an egg. The sun warms the earth. That, my dear, is the essential wisdom. In the very beginning as the Great Mother Lizard warmed the earth, rocks split open, mountains cracked, and the Giant Lizards, our First Ancestors, saw the light of the sun. Imagine, if you can, their gigantic proportions, their fiery energy, their tremendous strength. Continents were their playing fields. They flew through the skies and sported in the oceans. The eggs that they laid gleamed like domes on the world's horizons. They were the Mothers, the First Mothers; and all would have been well had the Mothers not asked the Supreme Mother for male companions. The Sun in Her bounty granted their wish. At first the little fellows were playful and happy, but in time they turned to mischief and turned the Mothers from the worship of the One. Then She grew angry. Her wrath was terrible. She punished the Mothers. And that is why, my dear, we have all been reduced to such diminutive proportions." The Old Lizard stopped. The Young Lizard squirmed. There was something about the story that he didn't really like, but what could he say? It was the Ancient Wisdom.

(1979–80)

From the Bedside Book of Nightmares (U. of New Brunswick: Fiddlehead/Goose Lane, 1984).

Having finished the fables, I thought I would explore the bloodier aspects of gay liberation and women's liberation — things to do with who one loved, how and why it hurt, and what about the family. Most of this work was done between '81–'83. At the same time, as a respite from the blood and guts of **The Bedside Book**, I also wrote **Aditi and the One-eyed Monkey**, a children's book for my niece, published in revised form in 1986. In the second half of 1983 I wrote **The Conversations of Cow**. The sense of audience which had been so exhilarating for the writing of **Feminist Fables** had become inhibiting. I felt pressure about toeing the party line. **Cow** was intended for my private amusement and for Christine's bedtime reading. I realise, as I write this, that in Christine I had found the Ideal Reader, a lesbian whose literary judgement and political awareness I respected. Writers need this.

It's obvious that for some time now I had been asking the question, what was my place in a world that often seemed absurd to me? All right, I was a lesbian, a lesbian feminist. But what was a lesbian? What was her relation to other people? And what about the problem of warring egos? Surely a cause, however just, had to be something more than the mere prevention of one set of egos from dominating another set of egos. (That's why Virginia Woolf in **Three Guineas** starts out with the question of how to prevent war.) In "Snapshots of Caliban" I tried to create a female Caliban, with a strong ego and a healthy appetite, who just wanted what she wanted. My conscious intention at the outset was to kill her off. But I couldn't. Perhaps no poet can. And I found that though its manifestation differed, egoism itself was as central to the voices of Miranda and

Prospero as it was to Caliban's.

I had known for some time that identity isn't only a matter of self-definition. It also depends on the identity that other people attribute to one. I played with the notions of identity and alienation in *Cow*; but there was an additional ingredient that entered into my thinking. Personal immortality is not one of the tenets of Hinduism, as it is of Christianity. Identity is arbitrary in the sense that who you happen to be this time around has to do with who you were last time around and who you wanted to be. Much depends, of course, on the level of interpretation of the metaphor of reincarnation; but the very framework makes it possible to ask: what would happen if one let go of the identity one clings to so desperately? I'm sure that question is an echo from my schooldays in Rishi Valley where the philosopher, J. Krishnamurthi, used to come and lecture.

But the problem still remains: as a creature, a lesbian creature, how do I deal with all the other creatures who have their own identities, or perhaps I mean their own identifications? It's apparent that the components of the core identity change from place to place and period to period. Today the main components seem to be based on gender, skin colour, and sexual choice, as well as other factors such as nationality and religion, which are more or less important in different places. Any threat to the sense of self causes a violent reaction. But then how are we all to live? That's one of the preoccupations of *The Blue Donkey Fables*; and also of my new book, *The Mothers of Maya Diip*.

SNAPSHOTS OF CALIBAN

I
Not wrong to have wanted you,
                    but wrong
should the desire, being thwarted,
                    turn to rage.
And there is rage.
              Cal, Cal, Caliban
threshes her limbs. For this –
                    pardon.
I and my creature
              must seek for grace.

II

So I summoned Caliban. She was
                    squat and ugly.
Sometimes she cried. Sometimes
                    she lied.
She was so sly and sometimes
                    so forthright
she disgusted me.
                    'Come, little Caliban,
I take you by the hand.
          We will walk upon the sand
to the bright, blue sea.'
                    But she knew
as we walked towards the cliff
          what fate I had in mind
and broke from me.
          And so, we run across the sand:
the little murderee
                    chased by monstrous me
trying to save herself
                    and me from me.

III
Suppose I came across her
        while she was sleeping,
her lips half-smiling,
           her body calm,
wholly absorbed in her dear dream;
or caught her staring,
        her ears prickling
to the strange sounds, the brave scenes;
or found her fishing
        in a cranny of the island,
unaware of the others,
        would I not like her?
Would I not speak,
      and approaching her slowly
try to make friends?
      Indeed, as I watched the monster,
would I not feel a monstrous grief?

IV

Outside his cell the children are playing.
"My sand-castle." "No, it's mine."
Caliban shouts, Miranda snivels,
she kicks the castle. Caliban howls
with bitter rage. Not very pretty,
these little children. They start
throwing sand. The sage emerges,
his lips curled in quiet distaste.
But the sun has come out. The children
are happy. The sage withdraws
to brood once again on the storms
he will cause, the tempest he'll make.

V *Caliban's Journal*

He has chopped wood (very badly too) and carried logs for one whole day. I have done it for 12 years. She pities him. When I tried to show her my own hands, she would not look.

* * *

They are playing chess. I could learn too. I am not stupid. But they say it's a game intended for two. They have left me out.

* * *

These berries are nice, those are not nice. This water is fresh. That water is salt. I learnt. I learnt all that all by myself, and I told it to them. They were so pleased. But one day when I said to myself, 'Miranda is nice,' and told it to her, she didn't like it. She told it to him. I was whipped afterwards.

* * *

M thinks that the new men are very like gods. What is a god? I think M is a god. When I told it to her, she said I was stupid.

* * *

Today I made friends with the new gods. They were quite friendly. One of them asked me if I would like to be a god. I said, "Yes." So they gave me a potion. We all drank it. I remember laughing. They said I would make a splendid god. I wanted to tell M that now I was a god, but I fell asleep.

* * *

P says I must try to be good. I said that I would try to try. I looked at M, she didn't say anything.

*   *   *

Some of the "gods" want to take me with them. But I no longer believe that they are gods. I don't trust them.

*   *   *

If they all go away, I'll be left alone. That might be nice. But I might be lonely. I shall keep a journal. Soon, very soon, I shall people this island (with nice people).

VI

There's something wrong with Caliban.
    Is it her shape? Is it her size?
If I could say that Caliban is stupid,
then that might help, but she can read and write
    and sometimes her speech is so lucid.
She does not feel? But I've heard her howling:
she howls like a dog or some tiresome animal.
    and she sobs at night.
Yet she is Caliban. I've seen her gaping
    at the blue heavens, or at me,
and I fear her dream. For there is something
I dislike so thoroughly about Caliban:
if she had her way, she would rule the island,
    and I will not have it.

They dreamed it. There was no storm,
no shipwreck, nobody came. Prince Ferdinand
was a rock or a tree. M dreamed it.
She said to the tree, "Bow gracefully,"
and the tree bowed with Ariel in it.
As for revenge – the old man's dream –
even in his dream he could not change them,
not utterly; they still plotted, still schemed –
as though in a play – until Ariel once again
was sent to intervene.
         And they never got away,
for here we all are, M and myself
and doddering P, still islanded,
still ailing, looking seaward
                for company.

All my pretty dreams smashed and broken. I hate Caliban. She did it. She did it the way she smashed my castles when we were both children. I shall speak to father. But father has retired to his cell again and will speak to no one.

Shall I speak to Caliban? I should like to tell her how much I hate her.

> Caliban, this is a hate poem.
> You are squat and ugly.
> You are not the noble
> > the beautiful other,
> You are part of me.

But that's wrong, very wrong. Not what I intended to write at all. I shall cross it out.

*   *   *

Caliban is ill. I can't help wondering if she is going to die. I do not want her to die. I am surprised. This thought surprises me.

*   *   *

Caliban says P poisoned her. P is upset. He is doing everything he can to try to cure her. We tried to move her into P's cell, but she says that she doesn't trust us.

*   *   *

C is unconscious. We moved her to the cell. P hovers over her like an anxious nurse. I do what I can.

*   *   *

C is recovering. Both C and P seem very ashamed. I also feel ashamed, but then, I have a reason.

IX *Prospero's Meditations*

Two monsters are crawling out of my eyes
and onto the sand, scrabbling and scuttling,
climbing and sliding on top of one another,
tipping over stones, doing themselves,
and one another too, some damage perhaps.
Of the two crabs which is more dainty?
Which one of the two least crab-like?
Most graceful? Is there a lovelier sheen
on one curved carapace, a subtler shine?
Their function escapes me.
                They have broken their claws.
Oh my pretty playthings,
                my shining instruments!

X
The fish in this stream
         are like the old man's thoughts,
         quick, dazzling, never still.
But that shadow over there – that's me.
And that larger shadow – that's him.
When his dream darkens
         it will swallow everything.

XI

He talked of dukes,
              palaces and peacocks,
fabled fountains, many such things.
He said I was a lady
             – it was my birthright –
fit for a king.
         From his superior knowledge
he made me a dream.
                  I listened
and understood clearly
             in myself I was nothing.

XII
The blue wave curves,
                    topples slowly.
I could banish the wave,
                    banish the sea,
destroy in a wink
                    this island paradise,
but something small
                    grovels within me.
I should like the sea
                    to be a slick blue.
I should very much like
                    this pain to subside.

XIII
When the monster loved me,
  she would catch crayfish,
take me to pools
    where crabs hid,
pluck berries,
     and gaze longingly
at my blue eyes.
      It was not
that I did not love,
   or could not love:
  I was often kind,
and I envied her
    her happy smile.

XIV

I dreamt last night that a huge tiger ranged over the island. It had iron insides. What it did not swallow, it destroyed by fire. It consumed everything. At last it came to the old man's hut and the little alcove where Miranda sleeps. "Caliban!" I heard them, I heard them screaming. I was inside the hut. I grew very angry. I hunted the tiger. I destroyed everything.

XV

Sometimes the airy substance of Miranda
is beaten so fine that I am the sky,
the air they breathe, the blueness of their sea.
I am so pure, so snow-white, I can take
any colour, fit any mould, be a bird
or a bush, a thing or a dream.
And then I know that it is my soul
and not my body that is stretched so thin.

XVI

M has confessed that it was she who poisoned me. I was very surprised. Then I was angry. Then I remembered the tiger in the dream. I started laughing. M looked puzzled. I explained about the tiger. I said to M that I would, if she liked, make a present of the beast. M looked startled. Then she grinned. We both started laughing. M said she had not intended to kill me entirely, she had just wanted to make me sick. (I am learning irony). I thanked her for it. She then explained why she was angry. P overheard us, but we were not able to explain it to him.

XVII *Prospero*

I made them? Maiden and monster
and then disdained them?
Was there something in me
that fed and sustained them?
Are they mine or their own?
I dare not claim them.

(1981–83)

The Blue Donkey Fables (London: The Women's Press, 1988)

Much of the verse in this book was written between 1983–84. I was tired after **The Bedside Book** and wanted the relief of immersing myself in aesthetic and technical considerations rather than political ones: that's why, for instance, I tried couplets and the sonnet form. I thought that if I could work on my technical skills, I'd have them ready perhaps when I wanted to tackle something more difficult. **The Blue Donkey Fables** themselves were written in 1986–87 at the request of The Women's Press.

Since my concerns here are with technique and to some extent with the effectiveness or ineffectiveness of poetry, this is perhaps the appropriate place to try and explain why references to **Gulliver's Travels** and to the two Alice books keep recurring in my work. It's easy to see why these books would be so congenial to me (as they have been to so many others) – the sense of the absurd, the satirical devices, the effective alteration of perspective and the subversive skills of "the outsider" – but there are one or two other reasons worth mentioning.

For me Swift was a great myth maker. Every line of **Gulliver's Travels** spills over with the inventiveness of his imagery. There's a sense of magnanimity and breadth of mind in Brobdingnag, an appreciation of the sheer physical beauty of horses in Book IV (even though this isn't simple appreciation and satire is piled on satire); delicacy as well as pettiness in Lilliput; and a wealth of patterns on which to base any number of dystopias in Book III. It's the exuberance of Swift that I respond to, of which the breathtakingly rapid satirical play is only one aspect. And if the giantess walks out of **Gulliver's Travels**, well then she walks out with all the splendour of her true stature.

The fact that Lewis Carroll was a mathematician is important to me. My original subject for the bachelor's degree was mathematics. I never took the degree because I didn't attend enough classes, and I was never really very good at it. But the thing about mathematics – in so far as I understood it – is that it makes beautiful patterns within self-contained systems. Jumping systems is disastrous. You get absurd results, because the axioms are different. In literature, on the other hand, some of the best results are obtained by using several systems simultaneously, though you have to be very clear about what you are doing. Now, it seems to me that Carroll understood the conventions of Alice's society perfectly, and had a great deal of fun playing with them. It's the skilful combination of patterns of logic, which are sometimes only patterns of convention, that gives such pleasure. That the White Rabbit and the other creatures, who are so alien to Alice, are nevertheless native to the world she has entered, may have something to do with my affection for them as well. I like the creatures, but then I like Alice too. After all, she tries to be logical and does her best to figure out the logic – or the lack of it – in the new systems thrown at her.

THE RETURN OF THE GIANTESS

There were the usual reverberations,
                               a racket
in the sky, birds squabbling
                      and swerving and mating,
fanfare of flowers, feathers
                            falling,
that sort of thing.
                      There were
the subterranean tremors,
                    the ambiguous weather,
hot and cold spells,
                and the unambiguous dreams.
That the return of the giantess
                  would be noiseless
and reticent was not to be expected.
                I had had warning.
But when she came, bending the green wave
of grass before her, treading the mountains
and – though courteous as ever – trampling
                    the hills,
and I opened my arms wide,
                 and wider
to receive her, neither grass, nor sky,
nor the pounding sea could hold her in,
and I held her close and we had our fill.

                                        (1983)

LOOK, MEDUSA!

Medusa living on a remote shore
troubled no one: fish swam, birds flew, and the sea
did not turn to glass. All was as before.
A few broken statues lay untidily
on the lonely beach, but other than these
there was nothing wrong with that peaceful scene.
And so, when the hero Perseus came to seize
the Gorgon's head, he thought he might have been
mistaken. He watched for a while, but she turned
nothing to stone. The waves roared as waves will,
till at last the hidden hero burned
to be seen by her whom he had come to kill.
"Look, Medusa, I am Perseus!" he cried,
thus gaining recognition before he died.

(1983)

THE ONE-EYED MONKEY GOES INTO PRINT

It was winter. The sun was shining like anything. It was pleasant, it was cool. The temperature was about seventy degrees. The one-eyed monkey was feeling mellow and middle aged. "I have travelled," she said. "I have seen the world. I have lost my tail, six of my teeth and one eye. I have lived. It's time I wrote down what I think about it." But her friends, the crocodiles, appeared not to have heard.

"Ahem," she said loudly. "I'm going to write a book."

"What for?" murmured one crocodile and went on dozing.

"What about?" muttered the other crocodile and went on basking.

She ignored the first crocodile and addressed the second exclusively.

"About me," she said strongly.

"Oh," replied the crocodile. "Will I be in it?"

"Well, I don't know," she answered. "Why would a book about monkeys have crocodiles in it?" But she saw that his eyes were beginning to close, so she added quickly, "But I'll put you in it."

"Me as I am?" he asked, stretching out his tail luxuriously.

"No, you as you are in relation to me."

"Oh." He sounded dubious.

"And you have to help me," she put in quickly.

"Help you to write it?" He sounded interested.

"No, no, I can do that. To tell you the truth I've already done it. I want you to help me get it published."

"Oh." He thought for a moment. "Well, I have

some contacts with the animal rights people. Send it to them and see what they think."

So she wrote to them and they wrote back that her title was lacking in human interest. That's what makes a book sell. People are interested in people, you know, they pointed out perfectly pleasantly. But they enclosed the addresses of a few publishers who were non-mainstream.

The one-eyed monkey had a crisis of conscience. Should she change the title? She changed it. It had been called *The Life and Leanings of a One-eyed Monkey*. She went through the text. Wherever the word "monkey" appeared she put in "blank". *The Life and Leanings of a One-eyed Blank*. She said it out loud. She persuaded herself that it had a ring to it. "I speak in parables," she told herself bravely. "The intelligent will know how to read in between the blanks and will appreciate my true, my native, my deliciously malicious monkey wit."

She sent it off to the publishers. Some wrote back and some misplaced it. Those who wrote back told her bluntly, "The syntax slithers and the vision is monocular. Who is talking to whom, may we ask? We regret to inform you that your work is entirely lacking in clarity." The one-eyed monkey felt disheartened. She brooded for days. Then she re-submitted the manuscript with the word "monkey" typed in clearly. And the miracle happened. A smaller publisher wrote to her saying that they were intrigued by her manuscript and would like to publish it. But please, they begged her to remember that an audience of exclusively one-eyed monkeys was hard to find; could she help to pay for it?

The one-eyed monkey tore her fur in utter despair. Her friends, the crocodiles, happened to notice.

"Oh, all right," they said. "We'll help you to

rewrite it."

"But it mustn't be about monkeys and it mustn't be about crocodiles."

"No," they agreed. They made suggestions and the monkey rewrote it.

In the end the book achieved a moderate success under the title *The Amorous Adventures of a One-eyed Minx*. "Is it autobiographical?" the reviewers wondered. "No," declared the monkey quite truthfully, "I do not recognise myself in it." But her publishers beamed. They patted her back. "Art transforms," they murmured kindly.

(1985)

THE VULGAR STREAK

The blue jay twittered at the Blue Donkey, "Birds are better." The donkey pretended not to have heard. The blue jay went on twittering, "Birds are better, better, better, much, much better." The donkey gave up. "Better than what?" "Than donkeys," the jay replied instantly. "Rubbish!" said the Blue Donkey. "Not rubbish. Just a fact." "Better at what?" asked the Blue Donkey, exasperated in spite of herself. "Better at flying," returned the jay. "But donkeys don't fly." "Exactly," cried the jay on a note of triumph, "that's my point," and flapping her wings, she took off.

All that day the Blue Donkey felt disgruntled. She tried to concentrate on important matters, but the jay's remarks kept coming back. When she caught herself wiggling her ears experimentally, she got really cross. "Well, so what if donkeys can't fly," she muttered. And she pulled herself together and made an effort and by the following morning she felt all right. But the following morning the jay was back.

"Wouldn't you like to fly?" enquired the jay. Now the Blue Donkey prided herself on being reasonably honest. What could she say? "Yes," she said. "But you can't," pointed out the jay. "No," said the Blue Donkey. "Too bad." And the jay took off. All that day the Blue Donkey was in a foul temper. Her friends told her that the blue jay was a flighty fool, not in the least worth bothering about, and in any case what did it matter that donkeys couldn't fly. "I don't care about flying," the Blue Donkey raged. "All I want is to teach that bird a thorough lesson." "But it's unworthy of you," her friends murmured. The donkey didn't care.

The next day when the jay returned, the Blue Donkey called out cheerfully, "I say, could you teach me to float?" "What?" asked the jay. "Well, flying's a bit strenuous for a beast my age; but if you could show me how to float, why then I could try it and practise in private." "What do you mean?" The jay was caught off-guard. "Well, you know, floating. When you just fold your wings and sit on air." Then the Blue Donkey looked at the jay suspiciously. "Are you saying you don't know how to float? Perhaps I'd better ask somebody else." "No, no," cried the jay. "Of course I can float. Look, I'll show you." And she flew into the air, folded her wings and plummeted to the ground.

The Blue Donkey cushioned her fall with a bundle of hay, but even so it was several minutes before the jay recovered. "Did I float?" she asked. The Blue Donkey shook her head. "Oh." "Would you like to float?" enquired the Blue Donkey. "Yes." "Too bad," and with that the Blue Donkey wandered off.

Afterwards the friends of the Blue Donkey reproached her. "That episode betrays a crude morality," they scolded. And it's at this point that they shudder involuntarily each time they repeat the tale. The truth is that the Blue Donkey had a vulgar streak. On this occasion she looked obstinate, then she glared, then she snorted. "Tell that to the birds," she said.

(1986–87)

111

Flesh and Paper (UK: Jezebel Tapes and Books, 1986; P.E.I, Canada: Ragweed Press, 1986)

In June 1984 I met Gillian Hanscombe at the International Feminist Book Fair in London. We corresponded. We wrote the poems in **_Flesh and Paper_** between 1984–1986. Many were taken out of the letters between us and woven into an inter-connecting text. It's not just that our identities as lesbians, our political awareness and our literary backgrounds corresponded; the structures of our imagination also corresponded, and this despite the fact that Gill grew up in Australia and I grew up in India. The logic of the text dictated that we not distinguish between who wrote what. In keeping with this, no distinction is made here. Section V consists of the poems we wrote after our visit to India.

That visit mattered a great deal to me. Now at last there was somebody in the West with whom I could talk about what things meant on the basis of shared experience. I had met other people who had been to India, but that wasn't the same thing. Gill had, at least to some degree, experienced the reality of my personal past (and continuing present, except that it's in a different bit of space). When one knows that someone else might be able to understand what one thinks, it's easier to think.

One of the unexpected effects of being in Gill's company was that I became aware of just how much I had been influenced by the Hinduism around me while I was growing up, and of the subtle ways in which a Hindu background rather than a Christian one shapes one's thinking. Before this, many of the other people I had talked with had known less about Christianity than I did. This was because Rishi Valley had been preceded by 5 years in a Protestant American boarding school in India. My parents' instructions had been clear:

112

"Learn what they have to teach you, but never become one of them." These instructions were quite easy to follow, since the school's interpretation of Christianity, in my opinion, did a disservice to its own religion. It was several years before I could read the Bible again with any pleasure. It helps to know what one is influenced by, even though one can't help being influenced.

There was another set of ideas that Gill helped me to clarify. I hadn't really thought about humanism much, except to say, "Look, women matter too." If pressed I'd have probably gone along with the vague humanism of the university atmosphere I was immersed in. It was only when I tried to imagine creating entire courses with a female literary tradition at the centre, and making these courses, rather than the traditional ones, the core of the English curriculum, that I realised that in the vague humanist terms I was used to, I would have been committing heresy. The implication of this was that humanism probably couldn't be separated from a male-centred consciousness. As for a feminist humanism, did I really want women separated from the rest of creation?

Many of these considerations have entered Gill's work and mine, even when we've been writing separate books. **Flesh and Paper** is of course a dialogue in its very structure. The two lesbians are trying to understand what kind of sense the world makes to a lesbian consciousness, and in the very process of writing are trying to deal with the fact that language creates worlds.

V
IN THIS KIND COUNTRY

Was it quite like that?

i
And so you said, "Well, which goddess then?"
I replied, "Come to the country of which
my bones are made up, I mean, the minerals,
the dust and ashes, the named chemicals. Our gods
inhabit birds and beasts and our ruined temples
are still functioning." So we went to India
where a stone is a god – if you say it is –
and where a great many stones are carved with
  gods,
but just lying about, because, as I told you,
the whole country is a gigantic junk heap.
When we walked about, both reverent and casual,
you were undisturbed. How shall I say it?
You were like me. Did you exercise caution
O my dearest love? You did not question my
  kinship.

ii
Was it quite like that?

We stop for coffee. No
tigers about. And the room air-conditioned. "The
context. . ." I mumble, break off inanely.
"Yes." You're businesslike.

"Your people show up badly here."

Is that it?
I'm white. I'm Western civilization. I'm Christendom,
their blood running in rivers. I'm capitalist
imperialism, overlording their lords. I'm
barbarism: misplacing, renaming. I'm us, not them.
"And the lesbians. . ." I try again. Mrs. Moore, alone
in the cave, lost her bearings. But that's a fiction
and the writer was one of us.

"We must go," you say gently. I make the coffee
taste just like home.

iii
But we were late for lunch. . .
                    My mother
might wait. In any event
                    all the servants
would be kept waiting. Why
                    make an issue
over time for coffee? Time
                    together –
that was the issue. But we were
                    together,
not face to face, side by side. . .
    And behind the explanations
the frightening admission:
            in this kind country
of exact relationships, there is
                    no word
for you and me.
            Come lover,
they are my kin
            and I their alien,
share the bloodied bonds with me.

They invent, circumvent

They invent, circumvent. No tigers here.
Lovers retreat.

At best they smile. They are seemly and courteous.
They sleep apart. Their goddess hides her face.
Shame has many modes.

The family takes trouble, infinite care. The
servants are kind and scrupulous. She does her
best to be a good guest, but has little to offer.
They do it for her lover's sake, who isn't her lover.
The gift of deception is hidden, implicitly prized.

Are they mated or parted? And do they know?

But you like what you see

But you like what you see,
        at least some aspects,
                some part of it.
I did not
        come into being
                a full-grown lesbian
with a knowledge of English,
            a trained brain
                and sexual politics
inscribed upon it.
        These native modes
                these shades of feeling,
return me to an element that feels
        like home.
                In the West I burn;
here,
        when my lungs give out,
                I cannot breathe.

I see what I can

I see what I can: monkeys, camels, an elephant,
untethered bullocks with painted horns; manhigh
shelters of tin, plastic, canvas, straw, timber, raffia
or mud; shrines, forts, temples, tombs, mosques
and palaces; bare hills, brown grass and crops of
the equatorial zone.

"There's a god," you'd said, "every 500 yards.
Often a rock painted orange."

We move about. Nobody stares. Only the hawkers
pester.

Sometimes you explain. "The cultures mix badly.
You ask and grab, we give and offer,
become more polite."

(If I don't belong, should I also not look?)
I finger my camera. "Be quick," you advise;
"people are shamed." (You want pictures of poverty?
Oh yes. Of itself, not belonging makes
me blind.)

At Mahabalipuram lies nine feet of Vishnu, on his
back and awake, sharing the last of seven temples
at the sea's edge.

Untutored, unenlightened, I do not shed my shoes.

In that particular temple

In that particular temple
                    a god slept
and a goddess danced,
                    and in another
a goddess slept and a god
                         danced.
Do I dare say it? Perhaps –
          it is possible –
that it's all the same?
                    That rapt
and dispassionate stare,
               the flaring curve
of the gorgeous hip
                    and the round
and unashamed breasts,
                    I have worshipped
before. When we make love
               you and I
are both sacred and secular.
               The goddess' limbs
begin to move.
               Balanced underfoot
the world spins.

Because of India

Because of India, before and after,
what could we uncover?
the history not for taking:
the family not for joining:
the cause not for naming:

and lover, what could we discover
in any country or poetry? (being

visitors; and seemly); we can

can

only take the goddess, carry her about,
plait for her a new liturgy (because

of India you came and I return). We can

– I/you can – press dreams and theories, bellies,
breasts, hair, hips, lips; and words; all
plaited now, until tomorrow. I have
told her, lover, to expect
fresh flowers for her feet.

We can compose ourselves

We can compose an ocean if we like;
deck it about with sand dunes, a
mountain or two, some trees.
Or we can compose ourselves.
But a politics? To invent, just we two,
a view? How to think? What to do?
And a country?
                    In yours, though the
climate is warm, the buildings fabulous,
though even the rocks have names,
we wither, having no word.
                            And in mine,
the word is so raw it bleeds; and from
fury of pain, it attacks; and would
maim us daily. We can compose ourselves;
but it's our bodies, not our passports,
fit so uncommonly well.

There is no undiscovered country

There is no undiscovered country,
   though the beasts are harmless,
      and the fish
  do not leap to tell us fiercely
         we must go elsewhere.
There is only an ordinary planet,
  where the shack falls down,
         weather prevails,
  and we must pay for safety
         with a disguised
  and difficult deference
        and the habit of fear.
And there is only a man-made language
      with its logic
 of need and greed,
       doom, dearth, despair.
But in spite of a hurtful history
  shall we speak of a peopled place
   where women may walk freely
      in the still, breathable air?

               (1986)

Afterword

The Mothers of Maya Diip, published by The Women's Press in the autumn of 1989, contains some verse and some fables, but it is on the whole a prose satire and that is why no extracts from it are included here. I've been living in Devon since May 1987. (This has been possible because the Home Office has special provisions for writers and artists.) I sent my letter of resignation to the University of Toronto in Oct. 1988. The line that keeps running through my head is from Section IV of **Flesh and Paper**: "Those/ women were translating verse into prose." In context it's not cynical, and I do not mean it cynically here.

I've set out these poems chronologically and offered some biographical information about what was happening to me and around me at the time, in order to indicate how, particularly for us as lesbians, the personal, political and poetic or intellectual development is interlinked. The process of trying to arrive at an awareness of how our thinking has shaped us is, in my opinion, more important than the particulars. If these notes prompt you to ponder on your own experience, then they'll have served their purpose. I've left out a great deal, of course, because of a shortage of space, as well as a reluctance to talk about personal things. There's an additional reason, which you, my fellow explorers, will understand only too well, and that is the unwillingness of people, however largely they may have figured in one's life, to be associated with such a book. For the time being, I take my leave of you on a Devon beach with two previously unpublished fables.

HALCYON DAYS

A kingfisher who had lived by the river mouth all her life long began to wonder if she had been missing something. There was the ocean stretched out before her. She liked to look at it, to watch its motion. She knew that there was a story about that when the sea is very calm, kingfishers build their nests on the waters – obviously absurd, but she liked the idea – it would be like living on a houseboat. She had occasionally ridden a log downstream, and that was the extent of her voyaging. She could dive – well, she could dive like a kingfisher, but as for floating, as for swimming, as for flying enormous distances, that was a different matter. Huge migratory birds sometimes flew over-head, but they never stopped to talk. It was the gulls who gabbled. "If you fly seven days and seven nights in a straight line without resting," one of them told her, "you come to an island where kingfishers are honoured." "How do you know?" inquired the kingfisher. "Have you been there?" "No," replied the gull, "but I had it from a friend who had it from a friend's sister." The kingfisher suspected that the gulls hadn't really been anywhere much. "This island," she said, "if it's so very far, how is it that they have any kingfishers?" "They're a rarity," answered the gull. "That's why they're honoured." Then the gull flew off and the kingfisher sat on her branch and pondered.

On that island, she decided, the lakes and rivers would flash and gleam with kingfisher colours. The fish in those waters would leap into the air and beg to be eaten. There would be signs on the beach saying clearly: KINGFISHERS WELCOMED AND HONOURED HERE. It might be a bit of a

125

nuisance being a celebrity. People might want to talk to her, they would want instructions on the best way to honour a kingfisher. She would have to make an appearance on high days and holidays and occasions of state even, when she might prefer to be away in the hills somewhere diving and fishing or perhaps only brooding. And then, of course, they might expect her to live up to her reputation – build nests on the water and that sort of rubbish. She looked around. A butterfly had settled on a lily pad nearby, an English sun filtered through the clouds making the blue of her feathers blaze, there were shadows in the river, fish lurking and hiding. Suddenly the kingfisher dived into the river and caught a fish. The scales of the fish glittered, drops of water fell in an arc. No one was watching. The kingfisher finished her meal peacefully. Then she dozed and dreamed of an island where kingfishers reigned and worked hard and controlled the turbulence of heaving oceans.

(1987)

PEBBLES

The kingfisher surveyed the pebbles on the beach. There was no sand at all, just pebble after pebble. She had seen people making a hollow in the pebbles, and knew that underneath the pebbles there were more pebbles, replacements so to speak, which would emerge to the surface should the need arise or the tides dictate. It all made her very thoughtful. If a gentle wave licked the pebbles and receded slowly, then for a few seconds the pebbles could be seen with great clarity, each shape distinct, and the markings and the colouring somehow lucid. Now, it was perfectly obvious that these heightened perceptions were significant, but the kingfisher couldn't quite define the nature of the significance; so the kingfisher said to a passing gull, "Look how the water seems sometimes to make each pebble quite individual." "What?" said the gull, and cutting the air with quick wings, flew on. The kingfisher decided that the gulls were probably very like the pebbles. They were like boulders, like larger pebbles, squatting on the beach. True, there were fewer of them and they flew about, but then so did the pebbles. The pebbles rolled and the sea rattled them.

Since the kingfisher couldn't understand the pebbles themselves, she decided to examine the words. "To be a pebble on the beach – what does it mean?" "It means to be of no consequence," she told herself. "It means to be like everyone else," she added helpfully. "And I am not a pebble," she whispered in parentheses. Meanwhile, another wave made another group of pebbles look very distinct. "If there were enough pebbles (and there are) and enough waves (and there are) and enough kingfishers on fulltime duty to look at them, why then every pebble, in a group or otherwise, would blaze blindingly at least for a second." This was a long sentence containing a complicated thought, and it had tired her; but she went on valiantly, "Would it not be possible to perceive the outline of each pebble without the help of a passing wave? I have eyes, I can see." "But be careful," she urged herself, "a systematic attempt to do just that could result in madness. My eyesight is good, but is it that good? I would have to be able to see everything and all at once and everywhere. And I would have to be wide awake. But I am a kingfisher. I am not – not somebody who can do all that." By this time the kingfisher was really exhausted, so she shut her eyes and dozed for a moment. When she opened them again, she sighed with relief. She was still on the beach, so were the pebbles, so were the gulls, and so probably was the significance, she decided; but it was all right, it wasn't necessary that she, an ordinary (though percipient and perspicacious) kingfisher, should have to go sleepless.

(1987)